Psoriasis Healing: From Curse to Blessing

Cover Designer: August Neverman V
Interior Designer: August Neverman V
Illustrator: Duncan Neverman

For more information to help you help yourself, visit Common Sense Home at:

https://commonsensehome.com

Contents

Introduction

When my skin erupted in 2015, I thought I was dealing with the "family curse" of inflamed skin that my mother had worn until she passed away in 2010. I went to a dermatologist; she said it was plaque psoriasis, and that I should learn to live with it.

When nearly half your body is covered in open, cracking oozing sores and you're in constant pain, "living with it" seems like a lousy option.

I started researching, and worked through diet, supplements, topical treatments and other remedy options until my skin was clear. I call it "mind-body-spirit" approach to healing psoriasis.

In this book, I take you through my journey. We'll also learn common trigger foods for psoriasis, and find out how to use herbs inside and out to help with healing.

We'll look at the connection between our emotions and beliefs and our skin. I believe that addressing this connection is critical to long term healing. We need to own our past and our present to move forward – whole – into the future.

I am not a medical professional, just someone who went through hell and came out the other side. I hope my journey can help others.

What is Psoriasis?

Psoriasis is a skin disorder that includes a buildup of excess skin cells, which often appear red and itchy, with silver-colored scales. Fingernail and toenails may be affected with pitting and discoloration. Scalp psoriasis resembles severe dandruff that may crust and ooze.

Plaque psoriasis is the most common. The thickened skin forms plaques (thick layers of skin) which can crack and bleed. Plaques may be small and isolated, or cover large areas of the body. This is what I was diagnosed with in 2015, but I have also dealt with inverse psoriasis and pustular psoriasis.

Pustular psoriasis includes tiny pustules (bumps filled with pus) and red, flaky skin. It most commonly occurs on the palms of the hands and soles of the feet.

Guttate psoriasis typically occurs in children or young adults, and is characterized by small, red dots, mainly on the torso and limbs.

Inverse psoriasis shows up in crevices, like armpits, groin areas and under the breasts. The affected areas tend to be red, shiny and itchy.

Erythrodermic psoriasis is an uncommon form of severe psoriasis that spreads quickly over large areas of the body with redness and shedding of sheets of skin.

There are more than 3 million cases of psoriasis diagnosed in the United States per year. One study published in JAMA Dermatology estimated annual expenses of psoriasis ca be as high as $25,796 per person, or $135 billion for everyone with psoriasis in the United States. Clearly, there's room for improvement.

The Year My Face Exploded

2015 was the year my face exploded. There was no C4 or dynamite involved, but it looked like I might have been a burn victim, and sometimes it felt like my skin was on fire.

It also scared me, as my mom dealt some sort of face rash in the decade leading up to her death in 2010. She saw over 20 doctors, and the relief she got was temporary at best. Her skin used to itch so badly that she would scratch her face raw in her sleep.

Was I destined to be stuck with something similar for the rest of my life?

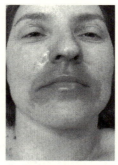

When I finally got a name for my condition – psoriasis – all the overpriced dermatologist had to say was to "smear some steroid cream on it and live with it".

I told her I was changing my diet to see if I could address the underlying cause. She flat out told me that I was welcome to try, but food didn't have anything to do with your skin.

Thankfully that doctor was wrong.

My Psoriasis Journey

Everybody likes to share and see happy family moments. Most of the time I stick to talking about the good times, too, but there were some bad times, and they left a mark.

My dad was an abusive alcoholic, and he beat mom while she was pregnant with me. My sister told me how he knocked mom down her knees on the concrete floor of the milk house one time when he got angry and she was very pregnant – but she still protected me.

My dad sued mom for divorce shortly after I was born, because she had the milk check put in her name so he couldn't drink it all up. He tried to force her to sell the farm and take the money, but thankfully the judge listened to mom's argument that she needed the farm to feed us six kids.

When my stepdad entered the picture seven years later, he did help mom with the farm and he didn't drink, but the man was still not a nice person. That's a story for another day, but let's just say that many aspects of my upbringing were less than idyllic, and that may have all played a role in bringing my physical problems to a tipping point.

Getting Sick, Even When You Try to be "Good"

When I was covered in oozing, peeling skin, I didn't want to talk about it, because I didn't have any answers. I was flat out miserable at times, and I felt like a failure.

My brother said to me at one point, "You try harder than just about everybody I know to do the right thing." And I do, darn it! But I still got sick and it took me quite a while to find something that helped.

I do my best to grow much of our food, and source much of what we don't grow locally and/or organically. I don't smoke, rarely drink – heck, I don't even drink much coffee. We don't eat out much, and don't buy much prepackaged food.

But we're not perfect. Sometimes when we're in the middle of big project, there will be frozen pizza for super. We like some sweets. (And sugar is the devil according to many current diet fads.)

I'm not binge eating boxes of bakery doughnuts, but I do know how to bake and am pretty darn good at it.

"You Need a Miracle"

That's what my neighbor told me when my skin was at its worst.

And she's right – I did need a miracle – but I already had one – my mother's love.

I figured if she could fight so hard to protect me, and stay strong emotionally at the end of her life, even as her body was being ravaged by the skin crap and myotonic muscular dystrophy, then I had to keep searching until I found an answer – for her and for me.

I wanted to find an answer for my readers, too. So many have offered suggestions for psoriasis treatment, and others have shared their own stories of dealing with chronic illness and being let down by conventional medicine.

Don't give up hope, and keep asking questions and trying things until you find answers.

Sharing My Story

I'm sharing what I found out during my research – looking for psoriasis causes, herbal treatments, alternative treatments, other underlying conditions and how I got my condition under control.

My skin started behaving oddly in early 2015, and the pain and disfiguration reached a peak at the end of the year. Early in 2016, I started seeing improvement, and by later in the year my skin was completely clear.

Since then, my skin has stayed clear, except for when my palms flared up in mid-2019 after I went off my thyroid medication. As of this writing (January 2020), I'm in good shape overall, although I do need to watch the palm of my right hand for dry skin.

My Mother's Story

Sharing my own problems with toxic skin wouldn't be complete without some background information on my mom's skin story.

Back in the late 1990's, she was diagnosed with rosacea, and given a prescription skin cream. This seemed to help for a while – until her face erupted into large red, itching welts.

What followed was a series of topical and systemic treatments that sometimes offered temporary relief and sometimes didn't help at all.

Out of all six kids, mom and I were the closest in build and general appearance, so I've always wondered if I might be more prone to skin problems as well. I guess I got my answer in 2015.

I was too late to help mom, but hopefully our stories will help others. I know she would want that, as she was one of the most giving, loving people I've ever known.

Toxic Skin, Years of Pain and No Answers

My mom lived on the other side of the state. During much of her illness, my husband was working two hours away and only home on weekends, so I was on my own much of the time with two young boys and a budding homestead.

I wasn't there for mom as much as I would have liked to have been. My brother and two sisters lived near mom and worked together to get her to appointments and see that she had help when she needed it around the old homestead. I was very grateful that my brother was just across the road on my grandmother's old place so he could watch over momma.

Mom's skin story started with the rosacea, as the official record goes. It developed into follicular lymphoid hyperplasia AKA lymphocytoma cutis or lymphadenosis benigna cutis, which is a type of rare pseudolymphoma.

It's not lymphoma, which is cancer that attacks the immune system, but resembles a cutaneous lymphoma in appearance.

DermNet NZ lists possible triggers:

• Tattoo dyes
• Insect bites
• Scabies
• Stings and spider bites
• Vaccinations
• Desensitization injections
• Trauma
• Acupuncture
• Gold earring piercing
• Infections with Borrelia burgdorferi (Lyme disease), Varicella zoster (chickenpox) and Human immunodeficiency virus (AIDS virus).

Of these, it's likely that mom was exposed to Lyme disease, insect bites, trauma, chicken pox, and vaccinations. There was also likely exposure to herbicides and pesticides during the years on the farm, which would be included in the general "foreign agents" description.

I also noticed that several of the medications she was one had skin problems listed in their possible side effects list.

Medscape notes: "The onset of drug-induced pseudolymphoma is insidious. Most patients present with a single slowly enlarging papular, nodular, or plaquelike lesion several weeks following the initiation of implicated medications.

However, several patients have demonstrated drug-induced pseudolymphoma after more than 5 years of therapy."

I don't know what caused her skin to go berserk, and the doctor's sure didn't know. Given that the skin is the body's largest elimination organ, I think her body was trying to purge something that was causing problems.

I know she had problems with edema (fluid retention) in her ankles, and that she had had an inflamed lymph node removed from her armpit area years earlier. She also had a history of bursitis – more inflammation.

Around the time her skin became inflamed, she was also diagnosed with myotonic muscular dystrophy (MMD).

I can't find the medical record related to the MMD, but she must have had type 2, because her mobility became more limited and type 2 commonly starts with muscles closer to the center of the body, such as the hips.

When she ended up in the hospital just a few days before she passed away, the doctors said that her guts had basically just shut down.

What if the two were linked?

I'll never know for sure if the skin and mobility issues were linked. I sorted through years of medical records, and nothing was mentioned about a possible link.

What I do know is that they tried a huge number of topical creams, hardcore antibiotics, immune system suppressors, oral steroids, and UV therapy. I even sent a copy of her medical records over to China to the family of our exchange student. They had a Traditional Chinese Medicine practitioner look at her skin condition, and sent back some topical creams for her to try.

Nothing cleared the itching and irritation for more than a short period of time.

But what if all of it was connected?

Poor elimination and slowed down digestive system could have easily contributed to a backup of toxins in her skin. She had multiple rounds of antibiotics, and very little in the way of probiotics. There's no way that her digestive and elimination systems could have been working well.

One symptom of this was the severe edema in her legs. Mom wore compression stockings for years, after suffering from phlebitis in middle age.

As she became less mobile, her ankles swelled so much they were as big as her calves, even with the compression stockings. There were also dark patches of skin, indicating poor circulation. Her lymphatic system was clearly not working properly to help clear toxins from her body.

My sister took mom all over the place looking for options. She saw some improvement after visiting a lymphatic massage therapist, who relieved some the swelling and improved the circulation in mom's ankles and feet.

There was also some improvement with the use of an ion cleanse machine, which would turn the water black each time she used it.

(I've used an ion cleanse machine in the course of my treatment, too. The first time the water came out black and green, but now it hardly changes color. Same water, but different me.)

Unfortunately for mom it was too little too late, but it did improve her quality of life. I still felt a lot of guilt for years that I couldn't do more. Yes, I was stuck on the other side of the state with two small children.

I didn't have any formal medical training, and as my brother pointed out, what's done is done. Feeling guilty can't change it. I still feel sadness and regret when I think about the situation. Hopefully our stories will help someone else.

Toxic Skin, Toxic Body?

I thought I was doing enough - eating "less bad", exercising regularly and working to reduce my stress levels. My skin was telling me otherwise.

Humans are complicated critters - made up of many critters (a healthy human body has roughly ten bacteria cells for every one human cell). Everything cooperates in a symbiotic dance to keep us healthy.

If you have visible symptoms – like skin conditions (even acne), swelling, bloating, dark circles under the eyes, funky body odor, flaky scalp, constipation, etc – then something is also not working where you can't see it.

We need to be our own advocates and listen to our own bodies.

When I went for my annual checkup in September 2015, the doctor also noted that down the road my psoriasis was likely to lead to psoriatic arthritis (where the psoriasis attacks your joints). That's not a path I want to take.

(Note: The National Psoriasis Foundation estimates that around 10% to 30% of psoriasis sufferers get psoriatic arthritis. This means that it's more likely that I won't get it. Thanks for nothing, doctor.)

It struck me as strange (and irritating) that the doctor was so matter of fact about something that was really screwing up my life and could possibly get even worse. I guess one develops a level of personal detachment over time.

Given than it was my health on the line, I had a more urgent and vested interest.

One of the first things I tried to figure out was possible psoriasis causes. I figured if I could eliminate the cause, eventually my skin would clear.

Psoriatic Skin Causes

Browsing around on the mainstream medical sites, they almost seem to "poo-poo" how psoriasis can throw a monkey wrench into your life.

Scaling skin is no joke. When my face was at its worst, I scared small children and got plenty of rude stares from people with no manners.

I'm not exaggerating. It looked like I had a mask over my nose and mouth area that burned a circular patch into the skin. One time I was waiting in line to get my thyroid medication, and I smiled at a baby that was looking over mommy's shoulder. The baby started crying.

Another time I was at a wedding of a friend's son. As we were standing outside the church after the service, I could feel eyes boring into me. I looked over, and there was a young woman staring as if I had the flippin' plague. She didn't stop staring until I commented rather loudly to my husband about some people being very rude.

It made me really uncomfortable to go out in public or do videos for the website. How could I talk to people about healthy living when something was so obviously wrong?

My skin would crack, bleed and ooze – just the slightest bump to an affected elbow would send pain shooting up my arm. I couldn't sleep at night because shifting in bed would break open the skin under my breasts and start it bleeding again.

Psoriasis can be a major life disrupter, and mine was small potatoes compared to some psoriasis photos I've seen on the internet.

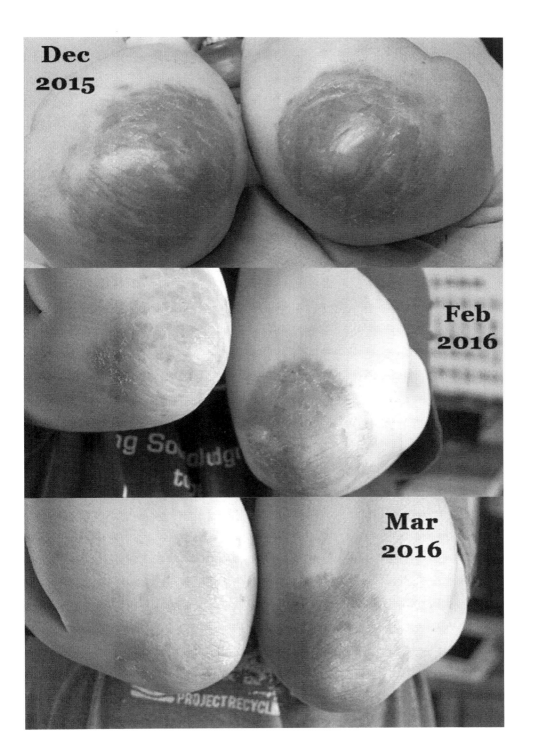

Mainstream Viewpoints

Here's WebMD's take on psoriasis causes:

> A variety of factors — ranging from emotional stress and trauma to streptococcal infection — can cause an episode of psoriasis. Recent research indicates that some abnormality in the immune system is the key cause of psoriasis.
>
> As many as 80% of people having flare-ups report a recent emotional trauma, such as a new job or the death of a loved one. Most doctors believe such external stressors serve as triggers for an inherited defect in immune function.
>
> Injured skin and certain drugs can aggravate psoriasis, including certain types of blood pressure medications (like beta-blockers), the anti-malarial medication hydroxychloroquine, and ibuprofen (Advil, Motrin, etc.).
>
> Psoriasis tends to run in families, but it may be skip generations; a grandfather and his grandson may be affected, but the child's mother never develops the disease.
>
> Although psoriasis may be stressful and embarrassing, most outbreaks are relatively harmless. With appropriate treatment, symptoms generally subside within a few months.

That sounds nice and simple, but doesn't match my experience. From what I've seen and what readers have shared, many of those with moderate to severe psoriasis suffer for years, even after trying various forms of treatment.

I did have frequent strep throat infections as a teenager (with accompanying antibiotics). A number of sources have linked strep throat to psoriasis.

I certainly have had plenty of stress in my life, including my mom's death, wrapping up our homeschooling years, and simply trying to find enough hours in the day to get everything done.

I didn't take any prescription meds except thyroid medication, and rarely use over the counter medications.

I'm not familiar with any family members who had psoriasis, although several family members have dealt with moderate to severe acne. Mom developed her skin problems the last decade of her life after a medication change. They changed her back, but her skin never calmed down.

Alternative Viewpoints

Contrast this with potential psoriatic skin triggers listed in "Healing Psoriasis: The Natural Alternative – The Drug-Free Program That Really Works", which looks at a broader picture involving gut health:

- Antibiotics
- Alcohol and caffeine
- Chemicals in processed foods
- Enzyme deficiencies
- Prescription corticosteroids (such as Prednisone)
- A Diet High in Refined Carbohydrates (candy, sweets, soda, white flour products)
- Prescription hormones (such as birth control pills and hormone replacement therapy)
- Mold and fungal mycotoxins (from stored grain, fruit and refined carbs)
- Chronic constipation
- Improper elimination

- Insufficient daily intake of water
- Foods high in saturated fats (I don't know that I agree with this one, as our brain is made up mostly of saturated fat)
- Nightshades – particularly tomatoes
- Smoking
- Negative emotions
- Depression
- Spinal misalignments
- Hereditary factors

In the book, "How to Heal Psoriasis from the Inside Out: An Energetic Perspective" the author touches on some physical causes such as:

- Having an acidic environment in the body
- Toxins and Heavy Metals
- Improper elimination/constipation
- Candida overgrowth

She also relates her own experience, where she found a connection between emotional/spiritual issues and her psoriasis, which is of course the primary focus of the book.

Particularly interesting to me was the section where she correlated reflexology points with areas of the body where the psoriasis developed. In my case, my psoriasis first showed up on my elbows.

The author notes:

> The inside of the elbows is a need to draw people or situations near to you, or to cling on. The outside of the elbow represents pushing people away.

She also notes that psoriasis on the front of the body relates to anxiety about what's ahead, which I have in abundance. I've also been anxious about my sons leaving (perhaps unnecessarily so, as they are in no rush to move out).

I've also been a rather private person most of my life, so I think that at times I struggle with the push to share more online with the website.

A German New Medicine Perspective on Psoriasis Causes

I discovered German New Medicine until 2019, when I had a secondary outbreak of psoriasis on my hands after the original outbreak had cleared.

I asked online friends if they knew of a good reference that correlated outward changes in appearance of skin, hair, nails, tongue, etc. with underlying issues. One friend recommended a Traditional Chinese Medicine textbook. Another suggested investigating German New Medicine (GNM).

German New Medicine originated with Dr. Ryke Geerd Hamer in the late 1970s and early 80s. Dr. Hamer was the head internist at an oncology clinic at that time.

When his son died after a gunshot wound, Dr. Hamer developed testicular cancer. Given his good health up until this point, it led the doctor to look more closely at traumatic events in patients' lives prior to cancer diagnosis.

What he found were clear patterns linking specific types of trauma with specific types of cancer. He also looked at patients' brain scans, and found that every disease was associated with changes in a specific part of the brain unique to that disease.

By addressing the emotional triggers associated with the disease, he saw excellent results with his cancer patients. They had a survival rate of over 90% after over 4-5 years, well above the rate of conventional medicine.

This was, of course, completely unacceptable to the medical establishment. They prosecuted him for the rest of his life. You can find any number of references referring to his work as quackery or pseudoscience.

I leave it at your discretion to decide if his theories have merit. For my part, each time I've looked up a chronic illness (mine or friends and family), I can readily identify the patterns that GNM associates with the disease. Psoriasis is no exception.

According to "Understanding Skin Disorders by Caroline Markolin, Ph.D.":

> Based on thousands of patients' cases, Dr. Hamer found that a skin disorder is always linked to a "separation conflict" which a person experiences as if "my child, my parent, my partner, my friend … was torn from my skin".
>
> …
>
> A Biological Special Program is in place to assist the organism in coping with this traumatic event. During the conflict-active stress phase, the skin loses epidermal cells causing a loss of sensitivity towards touch.
>
> The "sensory paralysis" is a natural form of protection from further traumas of this kind. As a result of the loss of epidermal cells, the skin becomes dry, rough, and may flake.
>
> **The resolution of the conflict is the turning point. Together with the healing that takes place on the psychological level, the skin also starts to heal by refilling and replenishing the ulcerated area with new cells.**

During this repair process, the skin becomes inflamed, itchy, blistery, and swollen. Skin disorders such as eczema, dermatitis, rosacea, hives, or herpes are therefore positive signs indicating that a natural healing process is running its course.

...

Dr. Hamer found psoriasis involves two separation conflicts. The active conflict shows as flaky skin, the resolved conflict shows red patches. The result is a familiar picture: silvery scales on a red surface.

Dr. Hamer discovered another biological rule:

He found that if a right-handed person suffers a separation conflict over a child or his/her mother, the left side of the body will be affected; if the conflict is over a partner (everybody except our mother or our children), the right side will respond. For left-handed people, it is reversed.

I think that one of the triggers of my psoriasis was working through the pain, guilt and loss I felt with mom's death. For my more recent bout of PPP (psoriasis on my hands), I've been dealing with other less acute feelings of loss. I'll talk more about this in the PPP section.

Candida

Candida – I didn't really know much about it, other than that it could cause yeast infections in your tucks and folds and private areas.

I had no idea that it would change my life forever – and may be affecting a lot of other people who knew as little as I used to know.

We're jumping around a little, but this is another critical piece of the puzzle. Remember – it's a mind/body/spirit solution.

In this section, I'm going to explain what candida is, what health problems may be linked to candida overgrowth and how I discovered candida was a problem for me. Then we'll tackle how to get it under control.

What is Candida?

Candida albicans (which I'll refer to as "candida" throughout this section) is a harmless yeast that lives naturally in your body. It lives in the gastrointestinal tract, on the mucous membranes and on the skin.

It's part of a balanced microbiome – all the microorganisms that work symbiotically with your body's own cells to keep you healthy. It is also sometimes referred to as a fungus – such as when a person gets a case of "jock itch". This is typically referred to as a "fungal infection", but it's due to yeast overgrowth.

Candida is harmless and normal – except when it isn't.

When candida grows out of control, it becomes pathogenic (disease causing). It sheds high amounts of mycotoxins (fungus related toxins) and the fungus can burrow roots into the gut lining, leading to leaky gut syndrome.

Leaky gut then contributes to toxins escaping into the bloodstream (instead of exiting via the waste cycle). This systemic fungal infection (candida overgrowth) is referred to as candidiasis.

What Causes Candida Overgrowth?

There are often a variety of factors that contribute to candida overgrowth. They include, but are not limited to:

- Antibiotic Use
- Steroids
- Birth Control Pills
- ERT (Estrogen Replacement Therapy)
- Poor Diet
- Chemotherapy
- Radiation
- Heavy Metals
- Alcohol Overuse
- Recreational Drugs
- Acute and Chronic Stress
- Amalgam Fillings
- Refined Carbohydrate and Sugar Consumption
- Excessive Dairy Consumption

As you can see, many of these factors are part of the daily lives of most people.

I had a mouth full of metal amalgam fillings. (I got these replaced one quadrant at a time by a holistic dentist in 2018.) I have also had pretty high stress levels in recent years, and was given antibiotics for a staph infection in 2015.

Something not mentioned on this list is kombucha consumption. Kombucha is brewed from a SCOBY – a Symbiotic Colony of Bacteria and Yeast. One of the yeasts that may occur in kombucha is Candida albicans.

This is not normally a problem, since (as mentioned earlier) it is part of a balanced microbiome. It might become a problem is if you drink large amounts of kombucha (which I did) and you have other risk factors in play (which I did).

Nowhere in the literature on kombucha that I read back when I started brewing was this risk mentioned, so I had no idea there was any risk at all. I still believe live culture foods are critical to good health – but there can be situations when you get too much of an otherwise good thing.

What Toxins Does Candida Overgrowth Produce?

Candida overgrowth produces toxic byproducts – over 79+ different mycotoxins. These mycotoxins attack the body and weaken the immune system. Here are just two of them:

•	Acetaldehyde – in excess, can cause brain fog and vertigo, create a thiamine and niacin deficiency leading to depression, fatigue, memory loss and more
•	Gliotoxin – deactivates critical enzymes that remove toxins and creates DNA changes in white blood cells that weaken the immune system

What Conditions are caused or exacerbated by Candida Overgrowth?

This list is adapted from "The Candida Cure: The 90-Day Program to Balance Your Gut, Beat Candida, and Restore Vibrant Health". It is a partial list only.

Autoimmune Diseases

•	Chronic Fatigue Syndrome
•	Fibromyalgia
•	HIV/AIDS
•	Leukemia

- Lupus
- Multiple Sclerosis
- Muscular Dystrophy (I wonder if this may have been part of what triggered my mom's MMD?)
- Rheumatoid Arthritis

Blood System

- Chronic Infection
- Iron Deficiency

Cancer

Digestive System

- Anorexia Nervosa
- Bloating/Gas
- Carbohydrate/Sugar Cravings
- Colitis
- Constipation/Diarrhea
- Crohn's Disease
- Dysbiosis (also called disbacteriosis)
- Food Allergies
- Heartburn
- IBS (Irritable Bowel Syndrome)
- Leaky Gut

Skin

- Acne
- Diaper Rash
- Dry Skin and Itching
- Eczema
- Hives
- Hair Loss

- Liver Spots
- Psoriasis

Respiratory System/Ears/Eyes/Mouth

- Asthma
- Bronchitis
- Dizziness
- Earaches
- Environmental Allergies/Chemical Sensitivities
- Hay Fever
- Oral Thrush
- Sinusitis

Endocrine System

- Adrenal/Thyroid Failure
- Diabetes
- Hormonal Imbalances
- Hypoglycemia
- Insomnia
- Over/Underweight

Nervous System

- Alcoholism
- Anxiety
- Attention Deficit Disorder
- Autism
- Brain Fog
- Depression
- Headaches
- Hyperactivity
- Learning Difficulties

- Manic-Depressive Disorder
- Migraines
- Schizophrenia

Urinary/Reproductive

- Cystitis
- Endometriosis
- Fibroids
- Impotence
- Loss of Libido
- Menstrual Irregularities
- PMS
- Prostatitis
- Yeast Vaginal Infections

Note: To be clear, this list is not meant to indicate that these conditions are caused solely by candida overgrowth. Many of them have a genetic component. That said, there is often an epigenetic component as well.

Most of us know that not everyone who has a gene that has been linked to a disease gets that disease. Something has to trigger that gene to become active.

This is epigenetics – the science that examines how environmental triggers interact with our genome. Many people have found that diet and lifestyle changes have sent diseases into remission, but this is not always successful for everyone.

The author of The Candida Cure was able to put her multiple sclerosis into remission through diet and lifestyle changes.

How I Realized Candida Overgrowth was a Factor in My Psoriasis

While I'd love to be able to say that the dermatologist who diagnosed my psoriasis mentioned a possible link between psoriasis and candida, she did no such thing. She never even mentioned that candida was a possibility.

Instead, she said it was likely some product I was using. (I use very limited products on my skin and in our home, and they are as non-toxic as I can get.)

She sent me on my way with a shopping list that looked like a Proctor and Gamble advertisement. (Proctor and Gamble received an "F" for Chemical Transparency in their products. They are not a company I care to support.)

She blew off my request to test for allergies, and when I directly asked her about changing my diet to help my skin, she said, "You can try, but what you eat doesn't affect your skin."

For a person with multiple medical degrees, she sure was awfully wrong. Of course, it's typical of far too many healthcare professionals in our current system. They get very little training in nutrition, and what training they do get is often inaccurate. Check out the processed low-nutrient food served on most hospital menus and this is quite obvious. "Let food by thy medicine and medicine be thy food" is completely out the window.

It turned out that I had a staph infection in the open skin on my elbow, so I was given antibiotics. I filled the prescription for steroid cream, and did use a little on my face leading up to the presentation I had to give at the Naval War College Strategic Studies Group in October 2015. (They wanted to learn about homesteading and self-reliance.) Meanwhile, I also tried out The Psoriasis Diet, with little change.

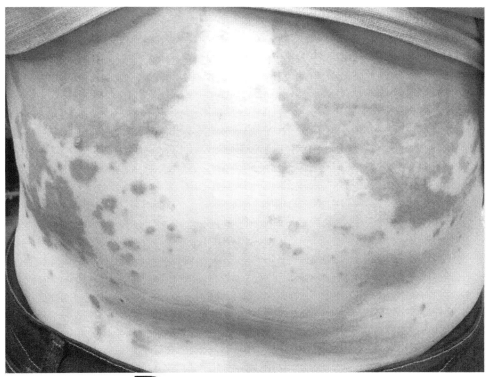

Dec 2015

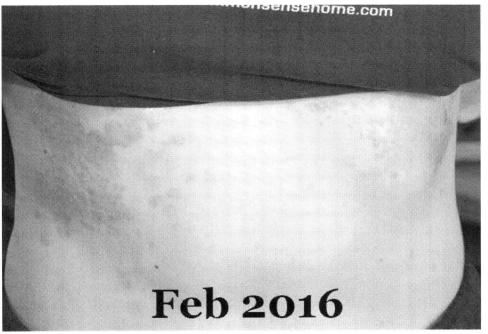

Feb 2016

When I got back from the trip to the Naval War College, I stopped using the steroid cream – and my skin went crazy. The steroids had only been suppressing the symptoms, not curing the cause.

I went in for allergy testing, hoping that something could be found that was a trigger. Results were good and bad – the few foods that registered as potentially problematic were, for the most part, not ones that I eat regularly. (Except egg yolk – I do like farm fresh eggs.)

Foods flagged to avoid included:

- Egg yolks
- Kidney beans
- Brazil nuts
- Kale
- Navy beans

Casein, cottage cheese, cow's milk, black beans, green beans, vanilla and pineapple were in the Moderate category.

There was no obvious "smoking gun" – except that candida levels were moderately high – which I didn't pay much attention to at first.

Time passed. Then I was discussing my skin with my friend, Casey. She looked at a photo of my face via Messenger and said, "That doesn't look like psoriasis."

All of the sudden, it clicked. I searched "candida overgrowth face", and saw an image that looked almost exactly like mine associated with the article, "The Curse of Candida".

BAM! Now that I had another piece of the puzzle, I could develop a strategy to heal. The candida and psoriasis went hand in hand. I wasn't able to clear one without addressing the other.

Easy Home Candida Test – The Spit Test for Candida

Are you wondering if you may have candida overgrowth? One of the simplest candida tests is called the spit test.

The testing is done when you first wake up in the morning, before you brush your teeth or get a drink.

1. Fill a glass with clean, filtered water at room temperature.

2. Spit gently into the water in the glass. (Just drop a nice spit gob in – no coughing up phlegm.)

3. Check the glass at 20 minute intervals for signs of candida, such as:

• Filmy "strings" hanging down from the split glob.
• A cloudy saliva film at the bottom of the glass
• Cloudy specs of spit suspended in the water

This test may produce false positives if you are congested or dehydrated, so it's best backed up with lab testing for confirmation. Lab tests can be run testing blood, stool or urine.

If you have a number of the risk factors listed above, your odds of candida overgrowth are much higher.

The Anti-Candida, Anti-Psoriasis Diet

My Anti-Candida, Anti-Psoriasis Diet was cobbled together from several different books, internet sources and trial and error. This has been working well for me, but every person is different, so listen to your body. Please check with your doctor or trained health care provider before making major diet changes if you have a serious medical condition or are on prescription medications. I don't often agree with doctors, but I don't want anyone doing something radical and somehow making their situation worse.

#1 – Avoid Allergens

Contrary to what the dermatologist said, diet did play a role in healing. What I've ended up with is sort of paleo-primal-ish, along with fermented foods and specific herbs and supplements.

I suspected my skin problems might be linked to some sort of allergic reaction to food. I ordered blood based allergy testing from Meridian Valley Labs (IgE and IgG4 antibodies) in mid-October 2015, and finally got the results back in late November.

The results were not what I expected. I had traveled to Rhode Island in early October, and had eaten foods I'd been limiting or avoiding (such as gluten) on the trip.

As noted earlier, the testing showed a significant reaction to egg yolk, kidney beans, Brazil nuts, kale, and navy beans. Grains (including corn and wheat) showed virtually no reaction, and other dairy products such as hard cheeses and yogurt were low.

Scrambled eggs and kale were a regular breakfast food, and I had been eating Brazil nuts for the selenium for my thyroid, but the other items were not foods I consumed on a regular basis. None of the foods were extremely reactive – they barely made it into the "avoid" range.

Even though they weren't flagged by the allergy testing, I still decided to stick with eating gluten free, and avoided dairy products for about a month. (It should be noted that all types of allergy testing can produce false negatives or false positives at times. They are not 100% accurate.)

I've since reintroduced limited dairy and gluten. I find I feel better and poop better when I eat mostly meat and veggies, with some fruit and limited grains and dairy. All our corn products (and most of our food) are organic to avoid GMOs and glyphosate contamination.

The "Big 8" Top Food Allergens in the United States are:

- Peanuts
- Tree nuts
- Milk
- Eggs
- Wheat
- Soy
- Fish
- Shellfish

These foods account for 90% of food-allergic reactions. If you suspect a food allergy might be part of your health problems (most people with health problems do have compromised digestion), it may be helpful to eliminate these foods for a time and reintroduce them one at a time to see if your condition changes.

In the book "Eating Alive: Prevention Thru Good Digestion", author John Matsen has four different groups of foods to avoid.

Group I is foods that he believes should be avoided by everyone. Group IV includes foods that may be a problem for some. Groups II and II are in between.

I include his list here because it may be helpful for some. I avoided groups I – III for about a month in the course of healing, and still limit foods from those groups.

Group I – Coffee, tea, chocolate, white sugar, alcohol, artificial sweeteners and preservatives, salt and tobacco

Group II – Baking yeast, peanuts, brown sugar, cow products and pork

Group III – Wheat, tomatoes, brewer's yeast and mushrooms

Group IV – Lamb, beef, chicken, turkey, eggs, shellfish, fish, soya, lemon, oranges, grapefruit, pineapple, apples, bananas, peaches, currants, raisins, apricots, strawberries, potatoes, squash, rye, oats, rice, corn, alfalfa, eggplant, carrots, cabbage, broccoli, cauliflower, celery, cucumbers, peppers, turnips, walnuts, cashews, brazil nuts, honey, maple syrup, molasses, raw sugar, curry, garlic, vinegar and onions

#2 – Limit Carbohydrates

Once I realized I was dealing with candida growth, I knew excessive carbs could cause trouble. Yeast loves sugar.

I didn't go extreme low carb, since that can cause trouble if you have an underactive thyroid. Insulin is needed to convert inactive T4 hormone into active T3 hormone, and very low carbohydrate diets naturally limit insulin levels in the body.

I eliminated snacks like chips and crackers, took only small portions of any sort of grains or potatoes, and pretty much ditched dessert. I eat my fruit apart from other meals so it digests quickly and moves on through without much time to feed the yeast. Veggies, meat and healthy fat make up the bulk of my calorie intake.

In a fine twist of fate, at the time I was working through my psoriasis, I was also finishing my bread recipes book – which required making all the recipes in the book so I could get good quality photos. At least the rest of the family and the neighbors enjoyed the bread.

#3 – Start the Day with Hot Lemon Water

Morning lemon water's becoming quite popular in a number of circles to help alkalize and rehydrate the body. I opted for the Eating Alive version, which calls for fresh squeezed lemon (for maximum enzyme content), warm water, and a small amount of natural sweetener.

I use about half a teaspoon of organic molasses for the magnesium content. Sometimes I also include a dash of cayenne pepper, but I don't enjoy the taste.

#4 – Chew Your Food!

This may seem self-explanatory, but digestion begins in the mouth, and we are a nation that often eats in a hurry. Wolfing down poorly chewed food makes the rest of our digestive system work much harder. Take the time to chew every bite completely and mix the food well with saliva before swallowing the bolus.

#5 – Intermittent Fasting

I'm not counting my calories, but I am watching when I'm taking in my calories. I decided to try intermittent fasting to give my body a longer period to rest from digestion.

It took about a week for my body to adjust. At first I had headaches and some fatigue. Now I've settled into a routine and it's pretty easy.

I try to finish supper by 7pm, and don't eat the next morning until after 10 am. Before 10 am, I start with lemon water between 7am and 8am, and medicinal herbal tea between 9 and 10am. Between 10:30 and 11am, I have a serving of fruit.

Lunch is usually between noon and 1pm, second dose of herbal tea mid-afternoon, supper between 6 and 7pm, and a third dose of herbal tea around 8:30 pm.

Dr. Mercola is also a proponent of intermittent fasting, and notes on his site that intermittent fasting promotes the following:

• Helps promote insulin sensitivity – Optimal insulin sensitivity is crucial for your health, as insulin resistance or poor insulin sensitivity contributes to nearly all chronic diseases

• Normalizes ghrelin levels, also known as your "hunger hormone"

• Increases the rate of HGH production, which has an important role in health, fitness, and slowing the aging process

• Lowers triglyceride levels

• Helps suppress inflammation and fight free radical damage

• In addition, exercising in a fasted state can help counteract muscle aging and wasting, and boost fat-burning.

I regularly exercise early in the morning while still fasting. My belly does start growling, but it's not that tough to hold out until after 10 to eat now that I've gotten used to it. If I was doing more heavy labor in the morning, I might have to shift my eating time earlier.

I did have some minor issues with headaches and fatigue the first week I switched to this schedule, but do not anymore.

Typical fasting times are 14-18 hours. Women tend to do better with the shorter fasting times, but each person is unique.

#6 – Use Herbal Teas

I rotate through different herbal teas to help kill off the candida, address inflammation in the body and flush out toxins.

From what I've read, candida adapts quickly to whatever you're trying to use to wipe it out, so it's a good idea to change your herbal tea every 7-14 days.

Teas that I have used for my Candida/Psoriasis:

•   Slippery elm in the morning with American Saffron tea at night, as suggested in The Psoriasis Diet
•   Red Clover Tea, as suggested in The Candida Cure
•   Essiac Tea, suggested by my friend, MaryJean
•   Numi 3 Root Tea with Turmeric, Ginger and Licorice
•   Dandelion tea
•   Burdock Tea
•   Pau d'Arco tea

I have also tried different anti-candida herbal tinctures and pills, but they made me constipated. Constipation slows down healing. You want to clear out toxins and anything else that is clogging up your system. The teas worked well for me, gently but effectively.

#7 – Include Probiotics

While you are fighting off candida overgrowth and working to rebuild a healthy microbiome, it's critical to send in beneficial microbes to rebuild your inner ecosystem.

Live culture foods can be wonderful, but sometimes the wild yeasts that are present may be too much for an already stressed immune system. Listen to your gut, or work with a trained health care practitioner who understands the connection between digestion and health.

While I was on my most restricted part of the diet, I avoided live culture foods. Instead, I tool probiotic capsules. Spore based probiotics can penetrate deeper into the digestive tract, making them exceptionally helpful.

In the book Brain Maker, Dr. Perlmutter explores fascinating connections between gut and brain health, and highly recommends the use of probiotics supplements and live culture foods.

In some severe cases, he even recommends probiotic enemas (with specific species of bacteria that are native to the lower intestine) or fecal transplants. It may sound crazy, but he has clearly demonstrated life changing results via a change in the microbiome.

#8 – Include Prebiotics

Along with the good bacteria, it's helpful to stock your guts with prebiotics, which are foods that the good bacteria need to thrive.

Inulin is a well known prebiotic, and it can be found in foods such as:

- asparagus
- leeks
- onions
- garlic
- Jerusalem artichokes (sunchokes)
- yakons
- chicory root
- dandelion root
- burdock root
- raw apple cider vinegar
- lemons
- limes
- unsweetened black currants
- unsweetened cranberries

Many other fruits also contain inulin, but are too high in sugar to eat in quantity while fighting candida overgrowth.

Gluten free "grains" such as amaranth, quinoa, millet and buckwheat can also feed good bacteria without the gut-irritating effects of gluten.

Note: If your guts are severely overgrown with pathogenic bacteria, it may be necessary to limit prebiotics, as they can also provide food for bad bacteria. This is explained in more detail in the book "Gut and Psychology Syndrome".

#9 – Limit Drinks with Meals

It's not uncommon for US residents to knock back one or more large (often sugar filled) glasses of liquid with a meal. This can negatively affect digestion, as it dilutes the digestive enzymes.

Instead of washing down half chewed food, take the time to chew more thoroughly and you'll find you have less need to guzzle down liquid. Sip, don't chug, and drink most of your daily water intake between meals.

Diet Change Heals from the Inside Out

For me, no topical psoriasis treatment that I tried had long lasting results – until I dramatically changed my diet. With the diet changes, my skin cleared, I lost weight, I had more energy, and an overall better quality of life.

Alternative Psoriasis Treatments

One of the most fundamental alternative psoriasis treatments I used was to change my state of mind.

When my skin went crazy, I was filled with a sense of hopelessness and despair. I knew that my mom's skin had become inflamed and caused her over 10 years of misery, and some of the best doctor's in the country had been able to do nothing lasting for her.

I have always been told how much alike my mom and I were, and I *knew* I was likely to endure the same fate.

After all, if over 20 doctors at Mayo Clinic couldn't solve the problem, what chance did I have? This mindset contributed to my misery, as I saw no future but one filled with suffering.

There's an old saying often attributed to Henry Ford, "Whether you believe you can do a thing or not, you are right."

When I believed it was impossible for me to heal, I created a feedback loop in my body, cranking up my level of problematic neurotransmitters and hormones – inhibiting the healing process. (It's also been shown that unhealthy gut bacteria further contribute to this feedback loop, which makes dietary changes even more important.)

There were two primary techniques that I used to address my mental health and get me on a path to healing – EFT (Emotional Freedom Technique) and BodyTalk.

I used a third technique – sound healing – to help with healing the 2019 flare up on my hands. Another option worth consideration is earthing, also known as grounding.

EFT (Emotional Freedom Technique)

I was introduced to EFT (also known as "tapping") in 2015 by a friend of mine who said they used it for stress relief and to help them stay focused. I ordered a copy of "The Tapping Solution for Pain Relief: A Step-by-Step Guide to Reducing and Eliminating Chronic Pain" in July 2015, and used it to eliminate my nagging lower back pain.

There are a series of exercises in the book that help you work through emotional and physical baggage that's accumulated over the years, let go of what's not serving you well, and rewire your brain for healing.

How Does EFT tapping work?

Tapping uses gentle "taps" on a series of meridian points around the body (the same ones used for acupuncture, reflexology, etc.) to rewire your body's energy system. I know this may sound a little strange to many of you, but tens of thousands of people have used it with good results – including me. At the very least, it should do no harm.

The concept isn't quite as odd as one might think initially, since quantum physics has shown that when you take things down to a subatomic level, we (and all matter) are made up of high energy particles.

I found that I had a number of "old wounds" that weren't really healed – anger towards my stepdad and others who were rotten to me, guilt that I didn't do more, and survivor's guilt. I think most of us manage to cram a lot of skeletons in the closet.

To go through a tapping sequence, you first start by choosing a problem to focus on and select a setup statement.

A setup statement is something such as, "Even though I have (this problem), I love myself wholly and completely." You then tap the "karate chop point" – the fleshly area on the side of the hand, and repeat this statement three times.

Now, tap 5-7 times each on the meridian points in the following sequence.

- Start of the eyebrow, near the bridge of your nose
- Side of the eye, near your temple
- Under the eye
- Under the nose
- The crease between the chin and lip
- The collarbone
- Underneath the arm
- Top of the head

As you tap each point, you say additional brief supporting statements, wrapping up at the top of the head.

In my case, when addressing my psoriasis, I might start with a statement like, "In spite of the inflammation of my skin, I love myself wholly and completely", and continue on with:

- the inflammation is leaving my face
- the inflammation is leaving my elbows
- the inflammation is leaving my torso
- my body is healing
- the candida is dying back
- my gut is healing
- the healthy bacteria are thriving
- my body is healing and I love myself completely

It sounds awkward, but I can tell the difference since I started using the technique. It's also simple and quick and you can do it almost any time and anywhere.

The Tapping Tree

To help you identify emotional targets that prevent you from healing, "The Tapping solution for Pain Relief" recommends drawing out a "tapping tree".

The tapping tree has four components:

The Leaves – Symptoms/Side Effects, your physical pain or emotional struggle

The Branches – Emotions, such as anger, shame, guilt, worry or other negative emotions.

The Trunk – Events that happened in your life that caused pain or stress, such as the death of a loved one or abuse, injuries, fights or other trauma.

The Roots – Limiting beliefs that hold you back and keep you from healing, such as "I don't deserve to be healthy" or "All I can do is live with this because there's no cure".

My tree parts were as follows:

Leaves – psoriasis, lack of focus, muscle pain, congestion, low back pain, can't get work done, fatigue

Branches – depression, anger, doubt, fear, sadness, frustration, insecurity, regret

Trunk – Mom's death, being abused by my stepfather, my husband losing his job and the possibility of losing everything we worked for on the homestead, being bullied as a child

Roots

"I've tried things to heal and nothing worked for very long."

"I am getting older, fatter and more miserable."

"The only direction from here is downhill. Don't get old!"

"I can't do more than I already am."

"I don't deserve success."

Labels within image: Muscle Pain, Congestion, Lack of Focus, Low Back Pain, Can't Get Work Done, Psoriasis, Frustration, Fear, Anger, Doubt, Regret, Fatigue, Depression, Sadness, Insecurity, Mom's Death, Abuse, Job Loss, Bullying, "I am getting older, fatter and more miserable.", "I don't deserve success.", "I can't do more than I already am.", "The only direction from here is downhill. Don't get old!", "I've tried things to heal and nothing worked for very long."

Dealing with Emotional Trauma

Much of my childhood was not very happy. My stepdad was a cold, autocratic man who was never satisfied. If I'd bring a report card home with straight A's, he'd ask why there was an A minus.

He didn't care for me having my own opinion, and regularly tried to beat them out of me. I guess I'm lucky that he didn't use a wrench across my face like he did my older brother.

By the time I left home I had a big chip on my shoulder and a low sense of self-worth. At the time, I couldn't wait to get away. Later, I had survivor's guilt, because I left my mom behind with that man.

As her health failed when she got older, instead of being a supportive husband, he spent more time away from home and left her behind. I firmly believe that at least some of her health troubles stemmed from loving a man who didn't know how to love her back.

On her death bed, instead of telling her he loved her or gently stroking her hair, he shook her roughly and told her she had to get up and go home.

I do believe he cared for her in his own way, but he simply didn't know how to love someone. It wasn't in him.

To compensate for feeling unloved as a child, I used to hoard candy – which led to me being a chunky kid. I also had thick glasses, and mom used to take me shopping at "the old lady store".

There was a rude comment that was popular when I was a kid – "You're ugly and your mother dresses you funny". That was me.

I still remember going to camp in junior high, sitting around one evening talking about whether the boys would try to sneak over to our bunkhouse. One of the girls commented, "Laurie is pretty". I knew she wasn't talking about me, because there was a petite blond in the group named Laurie. Still, I couldn't help but react slightly.

The speaker helpfully clarified herself, saying, "Laurie so-and-so is pretty".

That was my reality. I wasn't deserving of love, and I was ugly. These are things I knew to be true.

I often contemplated suicide, but decided I wouldn't give my harassers the satisfaction of beating me.

When I left home to head off to college, I thought I left that all behind. I found people who appreciated me (including my eventual husband) and there was no one nagging me that I wasn't good enough. Life went on. I got a degree, and another degree, got a job, got married, had kids and eventually moved out to our dream home in the country. Then things got messy.

Instead of getting promoted to head his department as expected, my husband lost his job of nearly 16 years. His employer moved to cut costs by replacing upper level management. I felt doubly betrayed, as they portray themselves as a Christian organization, but treated the people who gave the most to them like dirt.

He spent nearly a year freelancing and job hunting, until he found fulltime employment – 2 hours away. We bought a small condo for him to stay during the week, and he came home on weekends. I looked into selling our home, but the housing market was bad, and we would have never gotten the money out of it that we put into it. We struggled through five long years of living apart, never knowing how long the job was going to last because it was a contract position.

I felt hopeless, overwhelmed and deeply depressed. This is when my thyroid problems developed, which I get into in more detail is the Psoriasis on my Hands section.

My mom also passed away during this time period (January 2010). Instead of having time to grieve, I was immediately attacked over mom's estate. (I knew very little about her estate, given that we rarely talked about finances. They were a taboo subject for the family.)

There was a drawn out court battle, with bizarre incidents like my mom's ashes getting claimed as property by my stepsisters, and my brother threatening to sue me on behalf of an incompetent financial planner.

Over the course of the next several years, it led to estrangement from family members. My oldest sister blamed me for ruining her life. My stepfather and my oldest sister both died of cancer. I don't think I could process it all at the time, because it was so unexpected, bizarre, and overwhelming.

In 2014 my husband finally got a job back in the area, and we were able to start getting our lives and long term plans back on track. By the time 2015 rolled around, I suspect my subconscious finally decided it was time to deal with all the baggage I was still carrying around.

Over the course of mid 2015-2016, I worked my way around my Tapping Tree. I tapped on each area, working to release and clear the pain and negative beliefs.

I feel this was a very important part of my healing. Until I believed I could heal and deserved to be healthy, all the creams and diet changes had little effect. It was only after I began to forgive myself that dramatic changes started to happen.

Is this complete bullshit?

Consider this...

There are documented cases of people with multiple personality disorder (Dissociative Identity Disorder) where one personality has a disorder and another personality does not. For instance, one personality will break out in hives with exposure to strawberries, while the others don't react at all.

Perhaps one of the strangest episodes involved a person who had one personality that was diabetic, while the others were not. If one "genetic" disease can respond to belief, why not another?

Create your Tapping Tree, listing the symptoms, emotions, events and limiting beliefs that are causing you trouble. Work through each section – own it, and then let it go. It's all a part of what brought you to where you are today, but if it's no longer helping you, then it's time for new beliefs.

Our minds, bodies and spirits are connected. Like three legs on a stool, they give us balance and stability. Believe that healing is possible, and believe that you deserve to be healthy, and then take steps to support those beliefs.

I was looking through my notes from the time when my skin was at its worst, and found a "note to my future self". It read: "I won't have any crap on my face. Instead, I'll be able to smile without pain and have reasons to do so." If I can do it, so can you.

Another good resource for overcoming limiting beliefs is the book, "The Biology of Belief: Unleashing the Power of Consciousness, Matter and Miracles". It focuses on cell biology and the "why" behind how positive thought influences changes at a cellular level.

BodyTalk

If you want someone to help navigate through mind-body healing, BodyTalk may be right for you.

BodyTalk takes a whole person approach to healing, looking at physical, mental, emotional and spiritual aspects of the individual.

To use BodyTalk for healing, you need a trained BodyTalk practitioner. You can find a BodyTalk practitioner at https://www.bodytalksystem.com/practitioners/.

I've been blessed to have a dear friend who is also trained in a variety of healing modalities, including BodyTalk, MaryJean Bretton.

With MaryJean, no two sessions have been the same, because she sometimes uses the BodyTalk as a diagnostic tool and then uses other healing methods, and sometimes uses BodyTalk for the whole session.

I visited another practitioner, and their approach was different. They stuck to BodyTalk only for the entire session, and made some suggestions about food to avoid.

A "typical" BodyTalk session is described at Body Talk Central:

> A brief medical history is taken, identifying particular symptoms, pains or chronic health issues.
>
> Fully clothed you will be asked to rest face up, on a massage table. You will be kept informed of the formulas being used.
>
> Most people feel relaxed as they are asked to breathe deeply while the BodyTalk practitioner gently taps on the head and sternum (heart complex). The duration of a session is not indicative of the quality of the session or the results that occur.
>
> Because your innate wisdom is dictating the session, you can be assured of receiving exactly what is needed at that particular time for the enhanced communication and balancing to take place.
>
> A BodyTalk session itself usually lasts between 15-45 minutes. Your innate wisdom will dictate when the session is complete and establish a time when you need to return for a follow-up session.

BodyTalk is a complementary healing treatment, working to enable the body to help heal itself. It is used in combination with other treatments for acute conditions.

In my case, over the course of several months we worked on connections between the body systems, as well as emotional and spiritual problems. Although it was difficult to work through my problems at times, I feel like a burden was lifted from me.

Things got worse before they got better. In late 2015, I had large patches of raw, flaky skin all over my body. During a BodyTalk session, MaryJean said that she felt I would see major improvement in the next few months, and she was correct.

If we consider the process from a German New Medicine perspective, I moved from active conflict (flaky skin) to resolved conflict (red patches) to healing.

Sound Healing

My son, Duncan, took an interest in sound healing after a BodyTalk session with MaryJean.

The premise behind sound healing is that our bodies have a natural, healthy vibration frequency, which becomes disrupted over time. (All matter is made up of energy; all energy has a specific frequency or vibration.)

There are a number of different tools that can be used for sound healing, including tuning forks (weighted and non-weighted), Tibetan bowls, crystal bowls specifically for sound healing, sound tables, Rife machines and more. Natural sounds like bird song or ocean waves are recognized as relaxing or uplifting.

Duncan used a combination of weighted tuning forks and crystals to do spot treatment for healing and pain management when I was dealing with PPP (the psoriasis outbreak on my hands in 2019).

If you have alternative healthcare practitioners in your area who offer sound healing therapies, you may want to consider it as part of your treatment.

Earthing

Another treatment option you may find helpful is earthing, also known as grounding. Earthing places the human body directly in contact with the earth. The goal is to ground problem energy (as you ground an electric circuit), reducing inflammation.

Again, this relates to the concept of all matter is made up of energy. In our modern environments, most of us are subjected to a wide range of energy fields.

Some people are more sensitive to these fields than others. (Back when he was a computer repair tech, my husband ran into a woman who electrically shorted out any computer she attempted to work on, until they put her on a grounding mat.)

The simplest way to earth is to walk barefoot outside daily, for at least one half to one hour. If this is impractical, there are also earthing mats for chairs or beds that plug into the ground of an electrical outlet. This allows you to ground while sitting or sleeping.

In warmer weather, I run barefoot all the time, but I know that's dangerous in many areas. Duncan and I even make it a point to go out in the snow barefoot in winter. Getting outside and being active is great for getting the blood pumping and lymph moving, which also aids healing.

The book, "Earthing: The Most Important Health Discovery Ever" gives several examples of skin conditions going into remission after the use of earthing.

Topical Psoriasis Treatments

I found that in my case, until I changed my diet, topical treatments were only minimally effective. Even the pricey stuff prescribed by the dermatologist only took the edge off – but it did do that, and that bought me some time to make the changes that really addressed the underlying problems.

Early on I experimented with a variety of over the counter psoriasis creams, homemade herbal creams and essential oil creams, and different creams I could buy online.

As my skin started to heal, I switched to a soothing bath one or more times a week, in combination with spot treatment of irritated skin using different oils.

When my palms flared up in 2019, my skin responded best to colloidal silver salve with an aloe vera base, and argon oil. I still take a soothing soak at least one night a week.

Ditch Toxic Products

If by this point you haven't gone through your personal care products, perfumes, laundry products, cleaning products and anything else that might be in contact with your skin and switched to less toxic products, do so now.

Our skin is our largest organ, and it is permeable. When bad stuff gets in, it has to go back out.

Normally, waste removal is handled by lymphatic system, liver, kidneys and the rest of the internal cleanup crew. Unfortunately, we live in a toxic world, where products marked as "safe and effective" are often anything but.

Look for short ingredient lists that you can understand without a chemistry degree. Opt for deodorant instead of antiperspirant if possible, to let your armpits do their job clearing toxins. I found that as I changed my diet, my body odor was greatly reduced. More often than not, I don't use deodorant or antiperspirant.

There are a ton of online product guides available to help you find safer products. Be aware that many "natural" product companies, such as Seventh Generation, have been bought out by large corporations. Sometimes they maintain good product quality, sometimes they cut quality to reduce costs.

If you have a new flare up after using a product that has not been a problem for you in the past, try to check if the ingredients have recently been changed. (For instance, compare an old bottle of a product to a new bottle of the product. Sometimes "new and improved" isn't improved at all.) It can also be helpful to do a search on ingredients to determine if any of them are known to cause skin irritation.

Doctor Recommended Topical Psoriasis Treatments

As I noted earlier, the list of recommended skin care products given to me by the dermatologist consisted entirely of mainstream pharmaceutical products.

While I do think it's a good idea to eliminate toxic skin care and personal hygiene items, I didn't believe that this was my problem. I use very few products, and what I do use is non-comedogenic and non-toxic.

If this is not the case for you, you may want to change your skin care routine.

The main doctor recommended topical psoriasis treatments included:

- corticosteroids (to reduce inflammation)
- vitamin D3 derivatives (immune system moderators)

- coal tar extracts (reduces itching and scaling)
- anthralin (slows down the growth of skin cells)
- retinoids (vitamin A analogs that regulate epithelial cell growth)
- petroleum jelly
- phototherapy (light therapy)

Some of these are available over the counter (just hunt around at your local pharmacy for "psoriasis creams"), some of these are prescription only. Some of these can't be used in combination because one inactivates the other. Read labels, check with your doctor.

For scalp psoriasis, look for anti-dandruff shampoos or shampoos that are noted to reduce scalp inflammation, such as:

- Tea tree oil shampoo
- Neutrogena shampoo
- Aloe vera gel shampoo
- Neem shampoo
- Herbal shampoos for dandruff and dry scalp

Phototherapy is typically administered for stubborn cases or cases that cover a large area of the body. Psoriasis is treated with either UV-B (Ultraviolet B) or PUVA therapy.

As a therapy, these treatments are administered by a physician (although home UV units are available), but many people find their psoriasis improves with more exposure to plain old sunlight.

One of the doctor treatments that I did use for an extended time was petroleum jelly. While I normally avoid petroleum products on my skin, it's one of the few things that coated the cracking without causing more pain when my skin was really bad. This was a particular problem on my elbows.

When I asked at the doctor's office why they recommended it, the assistant said, "Because no one reacts to it." Fair enough, and true in my case.

Herbal and Essential Oil Creams for Topical Psoriasis Treatments

I was hoping that hard lotion bars would work for my psoriasis, but they didn't. I suspect that there may have been residual honey in my minimally processed beeswax that fed the yeast, but I'm honestly not sure. Whatever the case, applying the hard lotion on my active outbreaks made them worse, not better. This led to oozing, itching and more pain.

Friends of mine sent an assortment of herbal salves and ointments. I also tried some of my own, including plantain, comfrey, neem, dandelion and jewelweed. No luck for me, but perhaps your results will be better.

I tried my friend Gaye's "essential oil Miracle Cream with roller ball psoriasis add on" that she uses for her husband. It made me constipated with one application, and my skin burned. (Sorry if that's too much information.)

I have to be very careful with my use of essential oils, as even small amounts of them in carrier oils or creams often upset my system.

Coconut Oil, Tamanu Oil and Argan Oil for Topical Psoriasis Treatment

The two oils that I was able to use successfully for psoriasis treatment were coconut oil and tamanu oil.

Both of these oils have anti-fungal properties, so they are a good fit not just for soothing the cracked, dry skin of plaque psoriasis, but for treating the underlying candida overgrowth.

The downside of tamanu oil was that it leaves a sticky residue on the skin. Coconut oil isn't sticky, but can still be comedogenic, clogging your pores. It also takes some times to be absorbed by the skin, and can leave a greasy residue on clothing.

As I continued to do more researching, I discovered argan oil for skin care. Like coconut oil and tamanu oil, argan oil has antibacterial and antifungal properties. One of its traditional uses is to treat skin infections.

Argan oil is also non-comedogenic, so it absorbs cleanly and easily. Even though my psoriasis is clear now, I still use argan oil on my face and body as a gentle moisturizer when needed.

Do make sure to check the quality of your oil and find one that is well rated. I've purchased a few different brands over the years, and some were much better quality than others.

The oil should be clear, not cloudy, with a very light scent. If it smells bitter or strong, odds are it's gone rancid. Fresh oil will absorb quickly into the skin with no residue or tacky feeling.

As a bonus, argon oil is high in vitamin E, omega fatty acids and linoleic acids. It softens dry patches and can help reduce acne and fade scars. It's best to apply the oil on slightly damp skin after a shower or wash, to help retain moisture.

Warm Baths as a Topical Psoriasis Treatment

My weekly soak has been a source of great comfort. I also soak after BodyTalk sessions. I've read a number of stories of people who vacation by the ocean and found that the salt water cleared their psoriasis.

When soaking in the tub, use warm water, not scalding hot water. Hot water can dry and irritate the skin, making your symptoms worse. Several sites suggest 15 minutes, but I tend to soak a little longer. If I'm going to go to take the time to fill the tub with warm water, I'm going to make sure I make full use of it.

In addition to warm water, you may also find it helpful to add Epsom salts and/or Dead Sea salts to your bathwater. (I add both.)

Oatmeal is a well-known skin soother. You can buy finely ground preparations, such as Aveeno bath treatment, finely grind your own, or just put some oatmeal in an old sock and squeeze the milky oat liquid into the bathwater.

Some people add a small amount of oil to the water. If you choose to do this, don't use so much oil that you clog your pipes, and be careful not to slip getting into or out of the tub.

You can also brew an herbal tea using chamomile, plantain or green oat tops, and add the tea to your bathwater.

To brew an herbal tea for the bath, add about 1/4 cup dried herbs to 4 quarts of boiling water. Cover and let steep for at least 15 minutes. Strain out the herbs and add the tea to warm bathwater.

Those are the bulk of topical treatments that I've tried for my psoriasis. There are a ton of treatments out there, and I have by no means tried them all.

Psoriasis on My Hands
Palmoplantar pustulosis

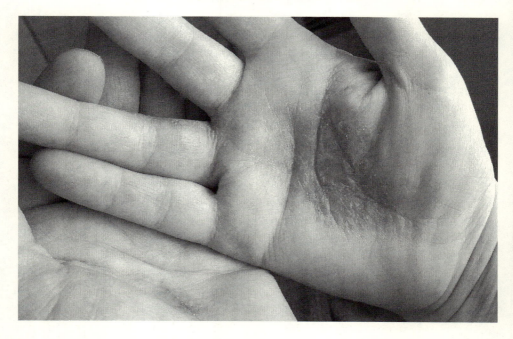

In 2019, I noticed an eruption of dry, flaky skin on my right palm. It grew to take up most of my palm, and spread up the side of my ring finger. My left hand also broke out, although not to the same extent.

I did not go in to the dermatologist to get an official diagnosis, given that she was so little help the last time around.

It appeared to be pustular psoriasis, possibly PPP (Palmoplantar pustulosis). At its most active, there were small blisters filled with white fluid in the affected areas, combined with flaking skin, oozing and itching.

In this section, I'll share the home remedies I tried, along with reader recommendations for other psoriasis treatments. Oddly enough, some of the topical treatments that worked well for my first bout with psoriasis didn't work as well for this flare up.

Why the heck do I have psoriasis on my hands?

In March 2019, I noticed a small red irritated patch on my right palm. I ignored it for some time, thinking that I had simply gotten into something that irritated my skin.

It took me about a month or more to realize what it was – pustular psoriasis. My "old friend" is back to teach me another lesson.

The National Psoriasis Foundation notes the following about Pustular Psoriasis:

Symptoms

Pustular psoriasis is primarily seen in adults. It may be limited to certain areas of the body — for example, the hands and feet.

Generalized pustular psoriasis also can cover most of the body. It tends to go in a cycle with reddening of the skin followed by pustules and scaling.

Triggers

A number of factors may trigger pustular psoriasis, including:

- Internal medications

- Irritating topical agents

- Overexposure to UV light

- Pregnancy

- Systemic steroids

- Infections

- Emotional stress

- Sudden withdrawal of systemic medications or potent topical steroids

Palmoplantar pustulosis (PPP) causes pustules on the palms of the hand and soles of the feet. It commonly affects the base of the thumb and the sides of the heels.

Pustules initially appear in a studded pattern on top of red plaques of skin, but then turn brown, peel and become crusted. PPP is usually cyclical, with new crops of pustules followed by periods of low activity.

Going through the Triggers checklist, the most likely culprits are stress and sudden withdrawal of systemic medication.

I'm Off My Meds

I've been on Armour thyroid since 2012, but decided to discontinue use is early 2019 due to a number of factors.

In the fall of 2018, I had a full body thermography scan, which showed no inflammation in the thyroid area. My thyroid tests have been largely stable for years. Antibodies were still high when last tested several years ago, but there was no growth in the lumps.

When I went to refill my thyroid prescription in January, the pharmacy switched me to Thyroid NP. It did not go well. I started having heart palpitations and my head was spinning and I felt messed up. I tried half doses and still felt like crap.

German New Medicine and Hypothyroidism

About this same time, I discovered German New Medicine (GNM). GNM linked autoimmune thyroid issues with feelings of helplessness – which is exactly the circumstances under which my thyroid problems started.

From "Hypothyroidism or Hashimoto's Disease at New Medicine Online":

> Hashimoto's is an inflammation of the thyroid ducts. In essence, it is a 'hanging healing' (PCL-A), where the healing phase has got 'hung up' due to ongoing conflict relapse.
>
> The hypothyroidism occurs when the efferent or outgoing thyroid ducts swell and occlude, thereby blocking thyroxin from entering into the bloodstream.
>
> If we can assist in a completion of the healing phase – thyroxin levels will return to normal. Otherwise, supplementation may be needed to avoid a condition known as myxedema, which involves a swelling of the skin and tissues.
>
> During conflict activity, the ducts will ulcerate (cell loss, cell negative) along with an elevation of "fight-or-flight" hormones. Only a slight tightness or pulling may be noticeable at this juncture.
>
> The intelligent purpose behind this widening of the duct is to allow for greater secretion of thyroid hormone into the blood stream in order to assist the individual to gain control of the conflict.
>
> Once the individual has come to terms with the conflict, the swelling or edema will occlude the duct, preventing the expression of thyroxin into the body.
>
> It is believed that the thyroid gland has become hypoactive or even non-functional – this is a misinterpretation. It is the swollen ducts that are lowering the thyroid hormone bio-availability.

Letting My Body Heal

Given my results on Thyroid NP, the lack of hot spots on my thermography exam, the GNM information (I don't feel helpless anymore since my husband has a job and I earn some income from the website) and the fact that my hormones are naturally shifting right now due to perimenopause, I decided to get off the meds and let my body do what it needs to do.

I have not taken thyroid medications since January, and have noticed no significant changes in general well-being – until March, when I got an itchy spot on my hand.

Resolving Conflicts with Losing Loved Ones

Recently, I have been very conflicted/saddened by the thought of losing so many that I care for.

If you recall from the earlier discussion regarding German new Medicine and psoriasis:

> Dr. Hamer found that if a right-handed person suffers a separation conflict over a child or his/her mother, the left side of the body will be affected; if the conflict is over a partner (everybody except our mother or our children), the right side will respond. For left-handed people, it is reversed.

My in-laws are aging. August (my husband) has been working long hours at work and it's taking a toll on his health. My siblings are dealing with more chronic health issues as they age.

I've been working with my BodyTalk friend to work through some of my emotional baggage. I think it's more than just loss of individuals; it's a loss of self.

We're becoming the oldest generation, and that is a heck of a responsibility. So many times I've looked to elders for advice, and I'm not sure I'm ready to be the elder.

I have been using EFT to tap on my fears and sadness about losing those I love. I won't say they are completely clear, but the rush of emotions has calmed a bit.

My Pustular Psoriasis Symptoms

For over a month (most of March and April 2019), all I had was a small rough patch of skin on my right palm. Then something kicked it into high gear, and I spent much of May and the start of June with pus-filled blisters, red, scaly skin, flaking, itching and oozing. The palm of my right hand and inside of the ring finger of my right hand had the worst symptoms.

The left hand had a small patch on the palm and some rough spots at the base of the thumb (on either side).

By early summer of 2019, the ring finger was clear, the left hand is mostly clear, and the right palm was much improved. Overall I was pain free and functional, with occasional minor flare ups of blistering and peeling.

By fall of 2019, both hands looked normal. As of this writing (January 2020), the left hand has been clear for several months. The right hand is a little bit dry and flaky in the palm and on the ring finger at times, especially after doing dishes or other rough work.

Treating the PPP

First off, I started watching my diet more closely, limiting sweets and potential trigger foods. Around 5/10/19 I started taking homeopathic thyroid support tabs to potentially help "bridge the gap" while healing.

5/16/19 I brewed up a batch of Four Herb Tea and started dosing again. Four herb tea, also known as Essiac tea, made the most noticeable difference in my skin when my whole body was impacted.

I'm also doing intermittent fasting, with nothing but a glass of green juice in the morning until around noonish (to give my body time to focus on healing instead of digesting).

I started taking Saccharomyces boulardii each morning on an empty stomach to crowd out any candida overgrowth, and a good probiotic at bedtime. The S boulardii was fermented in a batch of unsweetened berry puree, as suggested in the book, "Grow a New Body" by Alberto Villoldo.

January 2020

The last week in May, my husband, youngest son and I went on a "reboot" diet where we ate nothing but veggies in various forms via the program outlined in the book, "Grow a New Body".

I didn't notice a big difference, but my husband noticed significant changes in his health. (First he felt worse, then he felt better. He was finally able to ditch his sweetened drink habit and lost weight.)

Psoriasis Creams and Other Topical Treatments

I've tested different topical psoriasis treatments on my hands, to see what helped – and what didn't.

Calendula creams seemed to calm the skin down, but it also made it tender and a bit sore. Comfrey salve and plantain salve made the skin more bumpy, red and oozing. I had to stop with both. I tried neem oil, but it stunk and didn't seem to help.

Colloidal silver salve with aloe vera, plain CBD oil, EM-1 microbes, argan oil and witch hazel all seemed to help.

Coconut oil didn't help this time around. Last time when I had psoriasis all over, it was one of the few things I could use.

With the pustular psoriasis, I coated my hands in coconut oil after working in the garden one day, and the next day I had blisters again. I don't know why it worked one time and not the next, but when the flare up was active, coconut oil was a "no go".

Now that my hands have calmed down, I can use coconut oil again, but I've switched to argan oil for most skin care needs. I'm still taking Epsom salt baths 1-2 times per week to help with detox.

From Curse to Blessing

I was terrified when my skin got so bad (especially my face), but I've come to realize that it was a blessing in disguise.

You can't hide from something that stares at you in the mirror every morning. You can't apply enough anesthetic cream or take enough painkillers to ever be "comfortable" living your life to the fullest when your skin is raw and oozing and it hurts to smile or even breathe.

I was asked by my chiropractor, "Wasn't it hard to make such a big change?"

My response, "Yes, it was hard, but not nearly as hard is living in pain every single day."

My psoriasis forced me to face painful truths from my past and come to terms with them. It helped me to realize that I am stronger and more capable that I thought possible.

Healing my skin gave me living proof that a pronouncement from an "expert" isn't a death sentence. Experts can be wrong. They are humans, and they can only offer advice based on their experience and training.

Just like the rest of us, they don't know what they don't know. This doesn't mean they are bad people. Most try to do their best. It does mean that you can seek out a second opinion or other treatment options.

Living in constant pain also taught me to have a deeper compassion for the chronically ill. Of course we all do our best to aid and comfort those dealing with illness, but until you've dealt with something truly life disrupting yourself, you can't understand it in the same way.

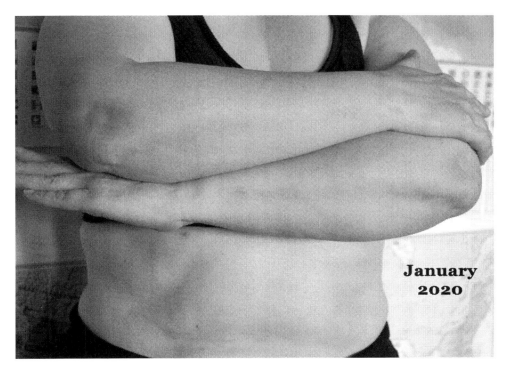

January
2020

I've learned to treat my skin as a diagnostic tool. Even now that the psoriasis is in remission, I watch for more subtle changes, like dryness or acne, and use them to help adjust my diet and self-care routines.

I now schedule time to take care of myself. Like many women, I tend to put my own needs last. Now I take a healing bath at least once a week, and use the sauna several times per week to help with detoxification. Rest and time outside simply enjoying nature (instead of always working) get put on the schedule – without too much guilt. Old habits are hard to break, but I'm working on it.

When we have internal problems like cancer or inflammation, they often go unnoticed until it is dangerously late. With psoriasis, the problem can literally be right in your face. We make changes, and we can see what works and what doesn't. It may be scary and miserable, but it's also obvious.

I hope the information I've gathered here helps you to heal, too. Psoriasis doesn't have to be a life sentence.

Readers' Thoughts

I put out a call to my newsletter subscribers to share their tips for dealing with psoriasis, and got a lot of feedback. I've shared their tips below.

Coni – "I have psoriasis on my scalp and a patch on my face. When it gives me issues, I use virgin coconut oil on my skin (wiping off any excess) and it seems to calm it down and go into a dormant state.

I always forget to keep doing it and with stress, it flares up again. Try coconut oil - that may be of help."

Marsha – "Please check out Clint Ober's free video on internet "THE EARTHING MOVIE".

He also has a second edition book EARTHING that has at least 6 citations on eczema and psoriasis."

Betty – "Laurie, my daughter and I both have mild cases of psoriasis.

She was the first to notice that hers was getting better each time she went swimming. Then I started paying attention and thought she was on to something. My guess is that something in the water treatment for our pool treated us, too.

Now that it's almost winter, my daughter has new psoriasis spots starting on her arms and legs. Mine have not shown up yet.

She's talking about finding an indoor pool to go to once or twice a week. She's convinced that pool water helps her skin."

Anonymous – "Aloe helps some, plus changing socks two or three times daily. Add plastic grocery bags over the feet if you have drying, cracking, and splitting. Keep your feet elevated as much as possible.

Add enormous amounts of vitamin B12 to your daily intake. Start with 1000 mg a day and work up to about 4000 mg a day. The liquid supplement seems to work best. Good luck. I've been dealing with this for 10 years."

Robert – "I've had a lot of trouble with skin problems. Right now I have horrible dandruff, perhaps, and psoriasis on my ears, inside and out.

I have tried Coal Tar shampoo, and it works for about a day for the dandruff.

For the psoriasis, I use Triple Paste AF. It helps somewhat. I have also used Aquaphor, with limited success.

I don't know if this is what you wanted to see, but here it is. I also have toenail fungus, big time, but have no solution for it at all."

Carolyn – "Several years and many moons ago I had a bad spot on my elbow. Being poor most of my life I tried home cures. This is before the internet and checking stuff out.

I scrubbed with baking soda and splashed with good apple cider vinegar. Hurt like you know what. I did this until the bumpy scaly skin was smooth.

The good news it was cleared up in less than 2 weeks and never had a big patch again. I still get tiny places and, yes, I use the same old cure.

I never went to the doctor so maybe not what you have had. No clue if this helps or not."

Mary – "My story:

I had psoriasis for a long time, it started sometime around 1960. It was awful, started on my foot, then on my head, near the hairline in the back of my head.

Years later, it attacked both thumbs. I scratched until they bled. I was going to a Dermatologist and getting treatment.

Fast forward many years, 1995, after finding out that my husband was having a long-standing affair, I filed for divorce. I went to see my Dermatologist for a different problem than psoriasis.

While there, I showed him my thumbs, NO PSORIASIS.

Jokingly, I told him that people who had psoriasis could dispense with his treatment and just get a divorce. He laughed.

I had not realized what a strain I was under from being married to a man who was a very smart person, but was unable to be a husband father.

Your email just reminded me of that and thought I would send you a laugh."

Faye – "I'm a naturopath and I'll share what I know from friend's experiences.

Sometimes it is a severe candida side effect (psoriasis), or other parasitic type or heavy metal poisoning and the body throws off through the skin. Detox diet can help a lot, and avoid too much sugar and eat a really clean, organic diet.

We should all be growing as much of our food as we can or sourcing from people we know, and visit their farms to see how they do it.

Our bodies need plenty of good oils, and a balance, animal sourced fat such as grass fed butter or meat, as well as Omega 3s. (Grass fed animals will have some Omega 3 in their meat or milk.)

Some vegetables have Omega 3 also, such as purslane and some of the dark green leafy things.

Good luck and God bless on all your endeavors."

Patricia – "I used to have a psoriasis issue, but it's all gone now, completely cleared. What I did may not be the kind of solution you're looking for, but it's what has worked for me.

First of all, aloe vera gel was helpful to put on the break outs, but what actually cleared things up was when I ran across a book by Valter Longo, PhD, titled "The Longevity Diet".

Don't be misled by that title: it's a medical protocol but they can't call it that (even though it's cleared up a number of dread diseases that currently plague people) simply because they lack sufficient medical trials.

The book is not long (about 300 pages), and actually is available for FREE (about $5.95 postage and handling) thru ProLon.com.

The "diet" protocol causes the body to go into 'autophagy', that is to stop burning sugars for energy and to turn to fats. (Fats, incidentally, are where the body tends to stash toxins and fake foods we feed it that it doesn't know how to process!) It's NOT a keto diet, not at all.

Anyhow, I began this protocol on my own in October of last year, and all the psoriasis lesions have disappeared and my skin is clear, no scaly spots, no itchy spots.

I guess it goes without saying that I have changed many of my food choices, but you could say it's the pattern of eating as much as the foods themselves that have 'mattered'.

The "diet" would be generally classified as "Mediterranean" and "Pescatarian". My weight has changed also, dropping from 230lbs to 165lbs since October of last year. This is happy news, although it's actually an unintended benefit of this protocol, not something I expected or set out to do. It just sort of "happened" on its own!

For anyone who has the discipline to take an active part in the care and keeping of their own body, I'd encourage them to send for the book (it's hardback, nicely done, and an easy read) and read it like there's no tomorrow!

Take notes, use note cards for suggested recipes, highlight passages and make notes in the margins. In other words, own that book and its message.

I don't know if any of this is what you were asking for, but here it is and I hope it will be a blessing to you and to others.

One last thing...

In reading the book it hit me suddenly: if this works with one dread disease (and there are many it has actually 'walked back') then it could work with ANY!

The reason for this is that the autophagy it precipitates also stimulates production of stem cells in the body! Think about that! Wow!"

Charlie – "I had psoriasis for 15 years. I asked several doctors what to do to "cure" it. Moistly they just laughed and said they did not know.

Five years ago, I finally got my head straight and figured out that I was low on vitamin D3.

Purchased a bottle of 1000 IU tabs and saw a big difference in 5 days. After 2 months, I was spot free; even the two spots on my legs that had been there for over 10 years.

Just wanted you to know what worked for me.

Good Luck!

P.S. On YouTube, kendberryMD has a couple of good videos on psoriasis."

Linda – "Yes, I've dealt with psoriasis for at least 10 years now, which means it didn't manifest until I was in my mid-60s.

I'll always wonder, why then? What was the trigger?

I suspect diet-and-lifestyle, the usual culprits, as I had put on some weight and was consuming more alcohol in that time frame. And, then, going on a strict AIP diet took off the weight and relieved most of my symptoms -- but not all and not permanently.

If there a psychological or emotional component to the breakouts/ flares, I've yet to make the connection.

I have two types of psoriasis: Inverse and Scalp. "Inverse" I find to be relatively easy to manage with steroid creams and diet, but the "Scalp" type is a lot trickier.

I'd love to find a better, long-term treatment. Does anyone have a good answer for scalp psoriasis?

An elimination diet (AIP) worked for me for finding my "triggers."

I've learned that I must limit sugar, grains and alcohol. I probably should avoid them entirely, but I don't. It's kind of a trade-off. I keep the psoriasis to a mild-manageable level, and I indulge in some wine, bread, dessert, etc.

My biggest worry: one auto-immune condition tends to pre-dispose a person to other auto-immune issues. That I don't want!

Not much help here, I'm afraid. I look forward to hearing more on the topic!"

Ramona – "Your story on psoriasis is what made me sign up for your newsletters because I have the same problem.

It seems though that my condition can flare up any time everything's not at optimum.

If the weather shifts, I get a breakout. If the temp changes, something erupts. My diet goes off and my scalp bleeds. (I'm currently pescatarian aiming for vegetarian/vegan because I noticed an excess of animal protein gives me the worst, longest, most painful breakouts.) Stress is also something I try to avoid.

Anything with strong chemicals triggers it too. It's a nightmare finding soap, shampoo, and even toothpaste I can use without my skin and scalp triggering. So, everything is natural and organic as I can get it, including my makeup!

Since psoriasis is an autoimmune disease, would my triggers just be for me? Do other people get reactions to the same things as me?

How do you best deal with the smaller lesions before they get worse? I hope we can help each other with this. I've had it all my life in varying degrees but nothing as bad as over the past 15 years (when I turned 30 seemed to be a turning point)."

Dan – "Anti-oxidants and edible oils. Feed the largest organ on your body from the inside."

David – "I've had psoriasis for about 30 years and 6 years ago was diagnosed with psoriatic arthritis (PSA). The rheumatologist told me that every person who has/had psoriasis will develop PSA. I take methotrexate to combat the PSA.

I'm fortunate that my psoriasis has never been very bad and now is only on one elbow and the bridge of my nose."

Richard – "A 1/4 CHEROKEE TAUGH ME TO USE 3 GALLON AUGUST COMPHREY LEAVES WASHED 3 TIMES IN WATER THEN SLOW SIMMERED IN 3 QUART OIL THEN STRAINED THRU CHEESE CLOTH. PRAY THAT JESUS WILL BLESS THE OIL. GOOD FOR NY SKIN PROBLEM."

Michael – "I have had trouble with psoriasis and it is so itchy. Don't scratch, because that will make it worse.

As far as medicine to use, it depends on what works for the patient. There are different kinds of medication, so a doctor might be good idea. I went to one, but he didn't really say what to get, so I got the cheapest anti itch cream with Hydrocortisone in it and a healing cream with coal tar in it worked the best for me. But that's just me!

I did try some others, but the coal tar did it."

Bob – "I have dealt with psoriasis for many years. I am fortunate in that, come spring time and being outside more, within a month or so into summer about 90 percent of the patches just fade away.

I don't take any medicine internally as don't like the possible side effects, and don't need another expensive medicine. Insulin is bad enough.

I do use a topical cream (triamcinolone acetonide cream) and that keeps it at bay, especially during the winter.

I have patches mostly on elbows, knees, some on butt and around belly button. I rarely have it on my face, and never had it on my hands. I go to the dermatologist twice a year to make sure no signs of skin cancer amongst the psoriasis.

In November I noticed I had more patches than I did last year. First thing I looked at was my diet. Based on experience, I cut back on red meat and nightshades, especially tomatoes. (I ate too many tomatoes from the garden in late summer and fall.)

That improved my skin quickly, several bigger patches getting lighter. The Pagano diet ("Healing Psoriasis - The Natural Alternative" by John Pagano) works well for me - if I can stick to it. The stricter I adhere to it, the better it gets.

We are traveling to Seattle for Christmas so will focus more on fish. I am originally from the Seattle area and was raised on fresh fish.

We get fresh frozen wild salmon and halibut from VitalChoice. They pack it in dry ice and we get it within a couple of days. We usually order in the summer when they have their sale."

Theodora – "I make a salve with plantain, comfrey, yarrow, and lavender, in a base of coconut oil, almond oil, vitamin E oil and beeswax."

Tizzy – "I have had great success using 10 drops each of frankincense, white thyme oil, and tea tree oil and Epsom salts in a warm bath and soak for 20 minutes.

I also mix the oils with an over the counter organic shea butter hand cream. Hope this helps you."

Laurie – "I had patches of psoriasis years ago. After researching, I used magnesium chloride (Ancient Minerals) oil topically for 3 months.

I used the flakes to make a saturated magnesium salt-water solution. I would rub it on my feet or anywhere else that it wouldn't itch when it dried. After 20 minutes, I washed it off.

It is claimed that after a shower or bath is a good time to put it on as the skin more readily absorbs at that time, but I never did this.

It cured my psoriasis with no return since. As a very surprising bonus, it healed a large cavity that I was dreading seeing the dentist over (she had shown it to me on the X-ray). When I went back to see her, my dentist found no cavities. I was shocked.

You have my permission to use this as it could help many with both issues and possibly more, as magnesium is an all-important mineral that the body needs but it so often lacking. Money often is too, especially when dentists are involved."

Basil – "As a child I can remember my grandmother in South Africa using aloe vera to treat all sorts of skin problems, including sunburn on my sister and me.

My wife of 56 years and I, also used the plant to treat our children and I know our grandchildren in Quebec and Ireland will have the same treatment when necessary. Between 80 and death I rub the gel on my face and hair most days with pleasing results.

Try it. You may be pleasantly surprised."

Katrina – "I suffered with psoriasis many years. The worst treatment for me was cortisone and most so called anti-allergy and baby creams.

The best relief was from royal jelly taken internally, and where it was really bad externally. I couldn't afford it for all places.

I also had baths in chamomile. I steeped a handful in a pan and poured it into the bath. (Never get the water too hot!)

I have been free for some years but when I have a relapse, Turmeric (1200mg with Piperine by Lumen) helps a lot.

I think a greatly overlooked facet, and probably a huge aggravator, is stress. If that's not treated, psoriasis is difficult to stop.

Soft clothing/sheets with cotton or silk can be helpful too.

It might be an idea to get the auto immune system checked for underlying causes. I've probably had Sjogren's syndrome for many years without knowing, until tested for other autoimmune problems. This provoked constant pain for days, weeks or months.

It's really important to try and do something positive. Learn something online, paint, write - and don't to be ashamed to talk about your troubles. People can't always understand if they don't know what you're dealing with, but there will always be those who are sadly uncaring.

Last but by no means least, family members often suffer with and for you and feel helpless. Be grateful when they try to help.

I hope this helps someone. It took me years to find the right help for my skin."

Lili – "My son has it. What worked for him is:

1) External applications of Castor Oil on plaques.

2) External application of 10ppm Colloidal Silver on plaques

3) Internal Probiotics

4) Turmeric taken orally

5) Magnesium Supplements internally and as Magnesium Oil on non-plaque skin"

Sindee – "I don't have a ton of experience with psoriasis or eczema, but I know we've helped a few people with our Cottonwood Balm (Balm of Gilead).

A nurse in Calgary said it helped so much when nothing else did, she took all we could spare, and several people I know have sworn it works. I'm not sure it works on everyone, or cures, but it sure relieves the symptoms, takes away the rash, the itch, the fungus under the nails.

We make our balm every spring, just the buds of cottonwood, olive oil and beeswax. For burns and bee/hornet stings, nothing we've used compares to it.

I don't pretend to know all about everything, I just know what I've seen, and how it really does work.

Just my little bit of experience...."

Rebecca – "My father and a woman in our church both had bad psoriasis for years. My father began using Herbal Fiber Blend (from AIM International), and the psoriasis cleared up. So, the woman in our church tried it, and her psoriasis cleared up as well.

For both, it cleared up within weeks. I recall both taking HFB for at least a year, but the psoriasis never returned, even after they stopped the HFB. This was at least 25 years ago. The woman has since passed in very old age, but my father is still living without psoriasis."

Home Remedies for PPP from Readers

After I posted photos of the psoriasis on my hands, our readers chimed in with home remedies for psoriasis that they use. I've gathered a number of them below. (Thank you to everyone who reached out.)

Natural Topical Treatments

Candice M. – "That looks like the stuff that's on my mom's hands. She used jojoba oil to help prevent breakouts."

Tom – "I have psoriasis that forms on top of my ears and in my scalp near my ears. I have been using a product called MG217 for psoriasis. It is a tar based ointment that works just GREAT. It doesn't cure my psoriasis, but it clears it up. It's very soothing."

Pattie – "Cortisone covered with Aquaphor and gloves will truly heal you faster. The Aquaphor softens and aides in healing. Coat your hands at night, and put white socks or gloves over the top to protect them. I cut off the toe of the sock, and a place for my thumb, like a fingerless glove."

chancie_cole (Instagram) – "I suffered from psoriasis for 16 years, and I found relief with a new skin care line that has cbd/hemp in the formula. It's changed my skin... BIG TIME!"

Sylvia – "Try Neem oil. It stinks, but it's supposed to help."

Maureen – "Look into Satya eczema and psoriasis cream. It's an organic and all natural Canadian product!"

Diet and Supplements

Meghan M. – "I'd purchase some MSM powder and add it to my morning smoothie. It's bioavailable sulfur that will get the inflammation of the hand problem under control.

My daughter had a hand that looked just like that, despite the fact that we were very healthy eaters.

A friend, who is also a veterinarian, gave her some MSM cream. Within days the symptoms were almost gone. Previously it had taken at least weeks to end a flare-up. MSM is really cheap so it's certainly worth a try."

Karon – "I realized that while at a beach house in Florida for my mom's 95th Birthday, my psoriasis cleared up in the week and a half. All I'd done different was take short walks on the beach.

Now, when I feel a flare up coming on I pop a 5,000 or 10,000 Vitamin D3 capsule for a day or so and it goes away before it gets bad.

My doctor said it works for some but not others."

mamamystic (Instagram) – "Have you read healing psoriasis the natural alternative by John Pagano? The diet he speaks about cleared me up so quickly." (Note – yes, I have tried this.

Shannon – "The only relief I have found is cutting out all white sugar, all grains, and white potatoes. Lydia Shatney put me on zinc and vitamin A which has also helped with healing. My skin would break out before and then not heal. Now it may flare a little bit, but I see it healing up really fast."

Lisa Marie – "Detox, eat a clean protein and veggie diet, and address digestive/gut health/microbiome optimization."

Jeannie – "Drink a gallon of distilled water in a day. Your skin will clear in 3 days."

Everything Else

Maureen M. – "I too have palmar-plantar psoriasis. I make my own goat's milk and aloe soap and a whipped shea butter moisturizer which I use every night.

I tried steroid creams and phototherapy and finally started Humira - which put me in the hospital with cellulitis in 2015.

One time my husband and I went on an Alaska cruise. My hands and feet were cracked and bleeding, and all I could think at the time was, "I will never enjoy this trip".

On one of our stops, my husband bought me a Philip Stein bracelet with natural frequency technology. I have been wearing it since.

It could it be coincidence – maybe - but I am no longer in pain.

The dermatologist even suggested I continue to wear it. I sincerely hope you read this and look into this technology, I truly believe it has helped me."

There are over 100 comments on Facebook alone, so I was unable to include every suggestion here, but hopefully these home remedies will help others.

Bibliography

Beaulieu, John. *Human Tuning: Sound Healing With Tuning Forks*. BioSonic Enterprises. High Falls, NY 2010

BodyTalk Central FAQ, http://www.bodytalkcentral.com/faq.php

Boroch, Ann. *The Candida Cure: The 90-Day Program to Balance Your Gut, Beat Candida, and Restore Vibrant Health*. Harper Wave, 2018

"Find a Holistic Dentist". Holistic Dental Association - Resource for safe metal amalgam filling removal. http://holisticdental.org/find-a-holistic-dentist/

"Hypothyroidism or Hashimoto's Disease". New medicine Online. https://www.newmedicineonline.com/hypothyroidism-hashimotos-disease/

Leavitt, Melissa. Psoriasis costs U.S. up to $135 billion a year. https://www.psoriasis.org/advance/psoriasis-costs-us-up-to-135-billion-a-year 2015

Lipton, Bruce. *The Biology of Belief: Unleashing the Power of Consciousness, Matter and Miracles*. Santa Rosa, CA. Mountain of Love/Elite Books, 2005

Markolin, Caroline. "Understanding Skin Disorders" Learning GNM https://learninggnm.com/SBS/documents/skin-new.html

Matsen, John. *Eating Alive: Prevention Thru Good Digestion*. Blaine, WA: Crompton Books, 1989

McKusick, Eileen Day. *Tuning the Human Biofield: Healing with Vibrational and sound Therapy*. Healing Arts Press. Rochester,VT 2014

Ober, Clinton. *Earthing: The Most Important Health Discovery Ever*. Basic Health Publications. Columbus, OH 2014

Pagano, John O. A. *Healing Psoriasis: The Natural Alternative*. John Wiley & Sons. Hoboken, NJ 2009

Panse, Guari. Cutaneous Pseudolymphoma Clinical Presentation. Medscape 2019. https://emedicine.medscape.com/article/1099188-clinical

Perlmutter, David. *Brain Maker: The Power of Gut Microbes to Heal and Protect Your Brain for Life*. New York, NY. Hatchette Book Group, 2015

"Psoriasis." WebMD. https://www.webmd.com/skin-problems-and-treatments/psoriasis/understanding-psoriasis-basics#1

"Pustular Psoriasis". National Psoriasis Foundation. https://www.psoriasis.org/about-psoriasis/types/pustular, 2019

Ortner, Nick. *The Tapping Solution for Pain Relief*. Carlsbad, CA. Hay House, 2015

Tallon, Dr. Ben. Lymphocytoma cutis DermNet NZ, 2006, https://www.dermnetnz.org/topics/lymphocytoma-cutis/

"Understanding Multiple Personality Disorders". Nurses Learning. https://www.nurseslearning.com/courses/nrp/NRP-1618/Section%205/index.htm

Villoldo, Alberto. *Grow a New Body: How Spirit and Power Plant Nutrients Can Transform Your Health*. Carlsbad, CA. Hay House, 2019

Manufactured by Amazon.ca
Bolton, ON

27066967R00049